**RED
BUSINESS
SERIES**

FAMILY CHILD CARE

Inventory-Keeper

The Complete Log for
Depreciating and Insuring
Your Property

Tom Copeland, JD

Redleaf Press®
www.redleafpress.org
800-423-8309

Published by Redleaf Press
10 Yorkton Court
St. Paul, MN 55117
www.redleafpress.org

Printed in the United States of America

ISBN 978-1-884834-76-9

Printed on acid-free paper

FSC
Mixed Sources
Product group from well-managed
forests and other controlled sources

Cert no. SW-COC-002283
www.fsc.org
© 1996 Forest Stewardship Council

Contents

Introduction

The *Family Child Care Inventory-Keeper* is an easy-to-use log that enables family child care providers to track the furniture, appliances, and other items they use in their businesses. Once you identify these items, you can reduce your taxes by depreciating them as business expenses. By filling out the *Inventory-Keeper,* you will have all the information needed to claim depreciation deductions for such items as a washer, dryer, computer, television, DVD player, refrigerator, stove, freezer, bed, sofa, lawn mower, microwave, swing set, and so on. You can use the *Inventory-Keeper* to claim depreciation deductions for furniture and appliances that you purchased years before your business began, as well as for items you bought after your business began. The *Inventory-Keeper* can help you identify many deductions that you may have otherwise missed.

Doubles as an Insurance Record

The *Inventory-Keeper* can also be used for insurance purposes if any of your items are ever stolen or destroyed. There is even a section where you can list items that are strictly personal. The *Inventory-Keeper* can track it all.

Useful to Whoever Does Your Taxes

The *Inventory-Keeper* can help you save money whether or not you use a tax preparer. You can give a copy of the filled-out *Inventory-Keeper* to your tax preparer, who will calculate your depreciation deductions for your tax return. Using the *Inventory-Keeper* will save you and your tax preparer time and effort. If you do your own taxes, you can calculate your depreciation deductions with the help of the step-by-step instructions in the latest edition of the *Family Child Care Tax Workbook and Organizer* by Tom Copeland. Either way, using the *Inventory-Keeper* can help significantly reduce your taxes.

Claiming Depreciation on Your Property Is a Simple Five-Step Process

Step One: Go through your home, identify the items you are using in your business, and enter each item in the *Inventory-Keeper*.

Step Two: Use the information from the *Inventory-Keeper* to claim business deductions on your tax return.

Step Three: Take photographs of the items listed in the *Inventory-Keeper*.

Step Four: Put the photographs and the *Inventory-Keeper* into the enclosed envelope and store it in a safe place away from your home.

Step Five: Update the *Inventory-Keeper* each year by recording when new items are purchased and when old items are sold, given away, or worn out.

Thanks to the following people for offering valuable input: insurance agent Peter Freisinger; tax preparers Kelly Nokleby, Carrie Campbell, Lorry Sorgman, EA, Sandy Schroeder, EA, Don Gilbo, and Marjorie Bergstrom, EA; and family child care providers Brenda Ives, Reva Wywadis, Deloris Friske, Marian Turner, and Michael Kauper.

How to Fill Out the *Inventory-Keeper*

Start in any room in your home, find the corresponding page in the *Inventory-Keeper*, and begin filling out the log for each item used in your business. Enter items that are not attached to your home and that you would take with you if you moved (such as furniture and appliances) on pages 17–49. Home and land improvements are items that increase the value of your property or prolong its useful life. They would stay with your home if you moved. Examples include ceiling fans, new roof, and a fence. Enter these items on pages 53–54.

Although it is to your advantage to list as many items in the *Inventory-Keeper* as possible, many providers do not claim depreciation on all of their items of lesser value, such as a kitchen clock or a wall hanging. There is no significant tax consequence for not listing such minor items. You can lump together a number of smaller items (kitchen utensils, linen, games, and so on) and report them as one item in the *Inventory-Keeper*. Keep a separate record that lists these items singly. Do not list any item you purchased after your business began that costs less than $100. Such items should be deducted in one year.

If your item does not appear in the *Inventory-Keeper*, record it on one of the blank lines for the room that the item is in.

If one of your items is not in the room as listed in the *Inventory-Keeper*, record it on one of the blank lines in the room where it does appear.

If you have a room that does not appear in the *Inventory-Keeper* (a third bathroom or a sunroom, for example), retitle one of the "Other Room" pages and list the items for that room there.

If you don't have one of the items listed in the *Inventory-Keeper*, leave the space blank. If an item wears out and you replace it, fill out the column "Year Disposed" for the old item and list the new item on one of the blank lines.

If you run out of space on one page, cross out items listed that you don't have and write in your additional items.

Items that are used only for personal purposes (china, antiques, personal dresser, jewelry, and so on) cannot be deducted as a business expense. You may, however, want to record these items on pages 56–59 for insurance purposes in the event they are stolen or destroyed.

Update your *Inventory-Keeper* at the end of each year. Add any new items acquired and indicate which, if any, items were sold, given away, or thrown out. If you give the *Inventory-Keeper* to your tax preparer, make sure you always make a copy for yourself and store it in a safe place away from your home.

Make sure that you always depreciate your home, because it is a significant deduction. When you sell your home, there are special rules to follow that are not affected by claiming this depreciation. See the latest edition of the *Family Child Care Tax Workbook and Organizer* for details.

How to Fill Out the Information for Each Item

Cost/Year Purchased: Enter the year the item was bought by you or the year it was received as a gift. Enter its cost if you know it. It doesn't matter whether the item was new or used at the time you obtained it.

Month/Year First Used in Business: Enter the month and year the item was first used in your business. If your business began January 1, 2009, and you owned the item before then, enter 1/09. Some providers may want to add the day as well.

Cost or Fair Market Value When First Used in Business*:*
Enter the lower amount of the original purchase price or the
fair market value of the item at the time it was first used in
your business. The fair market value of property you owned
for more than a year will almost always be the lower amount.
See pages 9–10 for information on how to estimate the fair
market value of an item.

Percentage of Business Use*:* You must choose one of these
three options for each item. Do not fill out more than one
box for each item. If you don't know what option to choose
because you are not sure how the item will be used for the rest
of the year, leave this section blank and wait until the end of
the year to fill it out. If an item is only used for personal purposes, list it under the "Strictly Personal Property" section on
pages 56–59.

- Time-Space Percentage—Put a check in this box if you
  use the item for both business and personal purposes.
  You will calculate your particular Time-Space percentage at the end of each year. The Time-Space percentage
  is a formula based on the percentage of hours and space
  that you use your home for your business. See the *Family
  Child Care Record-Keeping Guide,* by Tom Copeland, for
  details on how to calculate your Time-Space percentage.
  Note: For items used by your business and your family,
  you may also choose to use the actual business-use percent described below.

- 100% Business Use—Put a check in this box if you use
  the item exclusively for your business. Do not check this
  box if you use the item at any time for personal purposes.
  If you have a room that is exclusively used by your business (meaning no occasional personal use on evenings or
  weekends), all items in this room are 100% business use.
  If your own child uses the item only during the hours you
  provide child care, the item is still 100% business use.

- Actual Business-Use Percent—Fill out this box if you use an item extensively, but not exclusively, for business purposes. Enter the percentage of time the item is actually used in your business. For example, if you use a washing machine to do five loads a week for business use and three loads a week for personal use, your actual business-use percent would be 63% (five business loads divided by eight total loads). There is no one way to calculate an actual business-use percent. Some providers use a percentage based on the hours the home is used for business in a year divided by the total number of hours in a year. You must keep written records showing how you calculated your actual business-use percent. Because of this record-keeping burden, most providers who use items for both business and personal purposes choose to use the Time-Space percentage (see above) rather than the actual business-use percent. You can use the Time-Space percentage for some items and an actual business-use percent for other items. Most providers will find that it only makes sense to choose the actual business use percent for more expensive items that are used considerably more than their Time-Space percentage would reflect.

Year Disposed: Record the year when you give away or throw out the item. If you sell it, record the year and the amount received from the sale. The year an item is disposed is the last year you can claim depreciation on it.

Instructions for Other Pages

Summary Value of Your Items: A summary is provided on pages 50–51, where you can total up all your items under the Percentage of Business Use categories as they appear on pages 17–49: Time-Space Percentage, 100% Business Use, and Actual Business-Use Percent. In each case, add up the amounts in the column Cost or Fair Market Value When First Used in Business that correspond to the Percentage of Business Use category you arc using. For the Actual Business-Use Percent category, add together all items with the same percentage. After the first year you fill out the *Inventory-Keeper,* return to these summary pages to show the total of the new items purchased for each subsequent year.

Home/Home Improvements/Land Improvements: This section is where you should report these larger expenses associated with your home. See page 52 for details on how to enter these purchases.

Table for Strictly Personal Items: This section is where you can list items that are never used in your business. You cannot claim business deductions for such items, but by listing them in your *Inventory-Keeper,* you now have an indispensable tool for insurance purposes to help you determine the identity and value of your valuables and other personal items if they are destroyed in a fire or flood or are stolen. We have provided you with a sample list of strictly personal items on page 55. Enter the items you own on the blank pages (56–59). List the month and day purchased, the purchase price (or the value of the item if it was received as a gift), the serial number (for valuable items), and the room in which it is located.

Sample Table for the Family Room

	Cost/Year Purchased	Month/Year First Used in Business	Cost or Fair Market Value When First Used in Business	Percentage of Business Use (Choose only one)			Year Disposed
				T/S%	100% Business	Actual Business %	
Bookcase	$200/2007	1/09	$50	X			
Camcorder	$175/2008	1/09	$80			60%	
Camera							
Card table	$50/2004	1/09	$20		X		2009
Chairs	$250/2001	1/09	$100	X			
Clock	$25/2006	1/09	$5	X			
Clock radio							
Couch/sofa	$975/2001	1/09	$600	X			

How to Value Your Items

Take pictures of all the items you entered in the *Inventory-Keeper*. This will help support your estimate of its fair market value. For each item, do your best to determine a reasonable estimate of its fair market value at the time it was first used in your business. Use the lesser of how much a friend or neighbor would pay you for it or the actual cost to you. Do not use a replacement cost or the original purchase price if the item is more than a year old. There is no IRS-approved method to calculate this. As long as you make a reasonable determination of an item's value, you should not be challenged by the IRS. Here are some tips you can use to determine the fair market value of items:

- If you have the original receipt (or canceled check or credit card statement) or know the original cost for an item, you may want to reduce the original cost by ⅐ for each year that you have owned it (reduce by ⅕ for each year for a computer or printer). For example, if you bought a sofa for $1,000 in 2006 and started using it for your business at the start of 2009, you might estimate its fair market value at $570 ($1,000 - [$1,000 / 7 x 3] = $570). Look at the condition of your property to see if this is a reasonable estimate. Remember, you must use the lesser of the fair market value of the item, at the time you use it for your business, or its original cost. If you've owned an item for more than seven years, use perhaps 5% to 10% of the original price.

- Take pictures of your items to a local used furniture store and ask a salesperson what your items would have been worth when you started using them in your business.

- Estimate what an item would be worth if you tried to sell it at a garage sale.

- Look in the newspaper for the prices of similar items in thrifty want ads.

- Visit a thrift store in your area and base your valuations on their prices of similar items.

- Use the valuations from the software ItsDeductible, which is available from Intuit (it can be purchased independently or comes bundled with TurboTax). This software can also be used to estimate the value of clothing and other items given to charitable organizations.

How to Claim Business Depreciation Deductions

For items listed in your *Inventory-Keeper,* you can claim business expenses on your tax return using the following rules.

Items You Owned Before Your Business Began*:* You cannot claim a deduction for these items in one year. You must depreciate them over a number of years depending on what the item is. For example

* For computer, printer, scanner, and vehicle, use 5-year depreciation rules.

* For all furniture and appliances, use 7-year depreciation rules.

* For fences, landscaping, driveways, wells, and other land improvements, use 15-year depreciation rules.

* For home improvements and the home, use 39-year depreciation rules.

(If you began your business before May 1993, there were different depreciation rules in effect for the home and home improvements. The depreciation rules for all other items were different before 1987. Check IRS **Publication 534 Depreciation** for further information if you began your business before 1987.)

Items You Purchased After Your Business Began*:* If the item costs less than $100, you can claim this expense in the year you bought it. If the item costs more than $100 and lasts longer than one year, you must depreciate it under the rules described above. There is an exception to this rule. If the item is used more than 50% of the time for your business, you may use a Section 179 rule and claim the entire business portion of the cost in the year you bought it. This rule only applies to five-year and seven-year items. Warning: If you use the item less than 50% for your business in later years, or you go out of business before the end of the item's normal depreciation time period (five years or seven years), you will have to pay taxes on some of the amount you claimed under this Section 179 rule.

Depreciation rules are complex and subject to change. Once you start depreciating an item under one set of rules, you must continue using those rules for that item even if the rules later change. If you made an error in your depreciation calculations, you can correct this error in later years. For the most current information on how to depreciate items on your tax return, see the latest annual edition of the *Family Child Care Tax Workbook and Organizer*.

Is It Worth It to Depreciate All of My Household Items?
Most providers will find that it is well worth it to use the *Inventory-Keeper* to help them claim depreciation deductions for their business. Let's look at an example to see how this works.

You started your business in January 2009 and you listed the following items and their fair market value in the *Inventory-Keeper:*

Stove	$200
Refrigerator	$600
Washer	$150
Dryer	$200
Microwave	$100
Bed	$400
Freezer	$300
Swing set	$1,400
Sofa	$800
Dining table/chairs	$850
Total:	$5,000

We will assume that your Time-Space Percentage is 35%. The business portion of these items that could be depreciated is $1,750 ($5,000 x 35%). IRS rules require you to depreciate furniture and appliances over seven years (computers and printers must be depreciated over five years). Thus, you would claim $1,750 over the next seven years. On average, this would represent about $250 in business deductions each year.

$5,000
x 35%   Time-Space Percentage
$1,750
÷ 7   years
$250

The actual amount of depreciation deduction each year would vary slightly. Most providers would probably conclude that spending a few minutes recording these items in their *Inventory-Keeper* is well worth the approximate $250 deduction each year for seven years. Because your Time-Space Percentage can change each year, your depreciation calculation may have to be adjusted annually.

What If I Have Been in Business for a Few Years and Haven't Done an Inventory of My Business Items?
Fill out the *Inventory-Keeper* as soon as you decide you want to claim depreciation deductions on the items used in your business. Enter the lesser of the purchase price or fair market value of each item as of when you began using each item for your business. If you have been using furniture and appliances in your business for more than seven years (more than five years for computers and printers), then you are not entitled to any more business depreciation deductions on your current tax return. If some items have been used for less than seven (or five) years, you are still entitled to some deductions on your current tax return. The clock begins to run on claiming depreciation in the first year you begin using an item in your business. This is so even if you don't claim depreciation right away. For example, let's say you bought a refrigerator in 2004 and have used it in your business since then, but have

not claimed any depreciation until 2009. You have missed the first five years of depreciation deductions, but you can still claim it for the last two years.

Can Anything Be Done about the Past Years of Unclaimed Depreciation?

Probably yes. First, you can amend your tax return back three years and recapture your unclaimed depreciation by using **Form 1040X**. Or, second, you can go back further than three years and recapture your unclaimed depreciation if you file **Form 3115 Application for Change in Accounting Method**. To use **Form 3115** you must still own and use in your business the items whose depreciation from earlier years you now want to capture. By filing **Form 3115** you can claim all the previously unclaimed depreciation on your current tax return. This can help reduce your taxes significantly. See the latest edition of the *Family Child Care Tax Workbook and Organizer* for details on how to fill out **Form 3115**.

Other Tips

Photo Record

Take pictures of all items listed in the *Inventory-Keeper*. Take at least three or four photos in each room to make sure you have recorded every item. On the back of each photo, identify what room is shown and put the month and date the photo was taken. Put the photos in the envelope enclosed in the *Inventory-Keeper* and store them with the *Inventory-Keeper* in a safe place outside of your home (such as a safe deposit box). When you get your pictures developed, have a second set made to give to your insurance agent.

Videotaping

You could also make a video recording of your items. Take a tour of each room and record all business and personal items. Capture everything on tape by opening your kitchen cupboard doors and by showing everything in your closets and storage areas. You may also want to narrate your recording by describing your items in more detail. Keep a copy of the videotape in a safe place outside of your home. You may also want to make an extra copy for your insurance agent.

Insurance Coverage Problems

If items used in your business are destroyed by a natural disaster or are stolen, they may not be fully covered by your existing homeowner's insurance policy. Many homeowner's insurance policies only cover a limited amount of "business inventory" loss. For example, it may only cover $3,000 of the $7,000 worth of swing sets, playground equipment, toys, and children's furniture you own. If these items are destroyed, you would be responsible for the $4,000 difference. Providers who have accumulated a lot of items over the years or who don't have any children of their own living at home should be particularly concerned about having the proper insurance coverage.

Some policies offer no coverage whatsoever for any items used in a business. In addition, if you operate your business out of a building that is detached from your home (for example, a converted garage), your policy probably does not cover either the building or its content because it's considered commercial property. You will need to get a commercial insurance policy. Check your current policy carefully. If you are not fully covered, ask if you can purchase an insurance rider to obtain the necessary coverage. You may also want to see if you can get better coverage of your property through your business liability insurance policy. Every provider should have business liability insurance. Use an independent insurance agent to find a policy in your area (see the Yellow Pages). You may also call the National Association of Child Care Resource and Referral Agencies (703-341-4100) or the National Association for Family Child Care (800-359-3817) for the names of the local agencies and associations in your area that may be able to refer you to an insurance agent.

Operation ID

For personal or business items with a high value (or that are more susceptible to theft), you may want to mark them with a special identification number as part of the police department's Operation ID program. Keep a copy of the recording sheet given to you as part of this program and store it in a safe place outside of your home. Give another copy to your insurance agent.

Tax Tip

Keep track of all the time you spend filling out the *Inventory-Keeper* and taking photographs of your items. If you did this activity after the children in your care were gone, you may count these hours in your Time-Space Percentage. See the *Family Child Care Record-Keeping Guide* for details.

Dining Room

	Cost/Year Purchased	Month/Year First Used in Business	Cost or Fair Market Value When First Used in Business	Percentage of Business Use (Choose only one)			Year Disposed
				T/S%	100% Business	Actual Business %	
Buffet							
Chairs							
China closet/hutch							
Clock							
Curtains/shades/blinds							
Dinnerware							
Glassware							
Lamp							
Mirror							
Pictures/wall decorations							
Rug/carpet							
Silverware							
Table							
Table linen							
Wall shelves							
Window air conditioner							

Living Room

	Cost/Year Purchased	Month/Year First Used in Business	Cost or Fair Market Value When First Used in Business	Percentage of Business Use (Choose only one)			Year Disposed
				T/S%	100% Business	Actual Business %	
Bookcase							
CDs/cassettes/records							
Chairs							
Chest							
Clock							
Coffee table							
Couch/sofa							
Curtains/shades/blinds							
Desk							
DVD player							
Fireplace hardware							
Lamps							
Mirror							
Piano							
Pictures/wall decorations							
Pillows							

Planters																			
Radio																			
Recliner																			
Rocking chair																			
Rug/carpet																			
Stereo equipment																			
Table																			
Telephone																			
Television																			
Window air conditioner																			
Other																			

Kitchen/Pantry

	Cost/Year Purchased	Month/Year First Used in Business	Cost or Fair Market Value When First Used in Business	Percentage of Business Use (Choose only one)			Year Disposed
				T/S%	100% Business	Actual Business %	
Blender							
Broiler							
Chairs							
Clock							
Cookbooks							
Curtains/shades/blinds							
Cutlery							
Dishes							
Electric can opener							
Electric cooker/crockpot							
Electric juicer							
Electric skillet							
Food processor							
Freezer							
Glassware							
Microwave oven							

Item							
Mixer							
Pictures/wall decorations							
Portable dishwasher							
Portable trash compactor							
Pots and pans							
Radio							
Refrigerator							
Silverware							
Stove							
Table							
Telephone							
Toaster							
Utensils							
Wall shelves							
Window air conditioner							
Other							

Family Room

	Cost/Year Purchased	Month/Year First Used in Business	Cost or Fair Market Value When First Used in Business	Percentage of Business Use (Choose only one)			Year Disposed
				T/S%	100% Business	Actual Business %	
Bookcase							
Camcorder							
Camera							
Card table							
CDs/cassettes/records							
Chairs							
Clock							
Clock radio							
Computer							
Couch/sofa							
Curtains/shades/blinds							
Desk							
DVD player							
Fan							
Fireplace equipment							
Fish tank							

Games/puzzles						
Lamps						
Mirror						
Musical instruments						
Piano						
Pictures/wall decorations						
Pillows						
Ping-Pong table						
Radio						
Rugs						
Stereo equipment						
Tables						
Tape recorder						
Telephone						
Television						
Toys						
Vacuum cleaner						
Wall shelves						
Window air conditioner						
Other						

Play Room

	Cost/Year Purchased	Month/Year First Used in Business	Cost or Fair Market Value When First Used in Business	Percentage of Business Use (Choose only one)			Year Disposed
				T/S%	100% Business	Actual Business %	
Bookcase							
Camcorder							
Camera							
Card table							
CDs/cassettes/records							
Chairs							
Clock							
Clock radio							
Couch/sofa							
Curtains/shades/blinds							
Desk							
DVD player							
Fan							
Fireplace equipment							
Fish tank							
Games/puzzles							

Lamps							
Mirror							
Musical instruments							
Piano							
Pictures/wall decorations							
Pillows							
Ping-Pong table							
Radio							
Rugs							
Stereo equipment							
Tables							
Tape recorder							
Telephone							
Television							
Toys							
Vacuum cleaner							
Wall shelves							
Window air conditioner							
Other							

Master Bedroom

	Cost/Year Purchased	Month/Year First Used in Business	Cost or Fair Market Value When First Used in Business	Percentage of Business Use (Choose only one)			Year Disposed
				T/S%	100% Business	Actual Business %	
Bed/headboard							
Bedside table							
Blankets/bedcovers/ comforters/quilts							
Bureau/dresser							
Chair							
Chest							
Clock							
Curtains/shades/blinds							
Desk							
Fan							
Humidifier							
Lamp							
Linens							
Mattress pad							
Mattresses							

Mirror							
Pictures/wall decorations							
Pillows							
Radio							
Rug							
Sewing machine							
Table							
Telephone							
Television							
Wall shelves							
Window air conditioner							
Other							

Bedroom #2

	Cost/Year Purchased	Month/Year First Used in Business	Cost or Fair Market Value When First Used in Business	Percentage of Business Use (Choose only one) T/S%	100% Business	Actual Business %	Year Disposed
Bed/headboard							
Bedside table							
Blankets/bedcovers/ comforters/quilts							
Bureau/dresser							
Chair							
Chest							
Clock							
Curtains/shades/blinds							
Desk							
Fan							
Humidifier							
Lamp							
Linens							
Mattress pad							
Mattresses							

Item						
Mirror						
Pictures/wall decorations						
Pillows						
Radio						
Rug						
Sewing machine						
Table						
Telephone						
Television						
Wall shelves						
Window air conditioner						
Other						

Bedroom #3

	Cost/Year Purchased	Month/Year First Used in Business	Cost or Fair Market Value When First Used in Business	Percentage of Business Use (Choose only one)		Year Disposed
				T/S%	100% Business	Actual Business %
Bed/headboard						
Bedside table						
Blankets/bedcovers/ comforters/quilts						
Bureau/dresser						
Chair						
Chest						
Clock						
Curtains/shades/blinds						
Desk						
Fan						
Humidifier						
Lamp						
Linens						
Mattress pad						
Mattresses						

Mirror								
Pictures/wall decorations								
Pillows								
Radio								
Rug								
Sewing machine								
Table								
Telephone								
Television								
Wall shelves								
Window air conditioner								
Other								

Bedroom #4

	Cost/Year Purchased	Month/Year First Used in Business	Cost or Fair Market Value When First Used in Business	Percentage of Business Use (Choose only one)			Year Disposed
				T/S%	100% Business	Actual Business %	
Bed/headboard							
Bedside table							
Blankets/bedcovers/ comforters/quilts							
Bureau/dresser							
Chair							
Chest							
Clock							
Curtains/shades/blinds							
Desk							
Fan							
Humidifier							
Lamp							
Linens							
Mattress pad							
Mattresses							

Mirror						
Pictures/wall decorations						
Pillows						
Radio						
Rug						
Sewing machine						
Table						
Telephone						
Television						
Wall shelves						
Window air conditioner						
Other						

Hallways

	Cost/Year Purchased	Month/Year First Used in Business	Cost or Fair Market Value When First Used in Business	Percentage of Business Use (Choose only one)			Year Disposed
				T/S%	100% Business	Actual Business %	
Bookcase							
Chair							
Clock							
Curtains/shades							
Lamp							
Mirror							
Pictures							
Rug							
Table							
Other							

Bathroom #1

	Cost/Year Purchased	Month/Year First Used in Business	Cost or Fair Market Value When First Used in Business	Percentage of Business Use (Choose only one)			Year Disposed
				T/S%	100% Business	Actual Business %	
Bath mat							
Clothes hamper							
Curtain/shades/blinds							
Linens							
Mirror							
Pictures/wall decorations							
Rug							
Scale							
Shelves							
Towel rack							
Towels/washcloths							
Other							

Bathroom #2

	Cost/Year Purchased	Month/Year First Used in Business	Cost or Fair Market Value When First Used in Business	Percentage of Business Use (Choose only one)			Year Disposed
				T/S%	100% Business	Actual Business %	
Clothes hamper							
Curtain/shades/blinds							
Linens							
Mirror							
Pictures/wall decorations							
Rug							
Scale							
Shelves							
Towel rack							
Towels/washcloths							
Other							

Office

	Cost/Year Purchased	Month/Year First Used in Business	Cost or Fair Market Value When First Used in Business	Percentage of Business Use (Choose only one)			Year Disposed
				T/S%	100% Business	Actual Business %	
Bookcase							
Chair							
Computer							
Desk							
Fax							
File cabinets							
Photocopier							
Printer							
Scanner							
Table							
Typewriter							
Wall shelves							
Window air conditioner							
Other							

Entryway

	Cost/Year Purchased	Month/Year First Used in Business	Cost or Fair Market Value When First Used in Business	Percentage of Business Use (Choose only one)			Year Disposed
				T/S%	100% Business	Actual Business %	
Carpet sweeper							
Chair							
Clock							
Curtains/shades							
Hats/mittens/gloves							
Lamp							
Mirror							
Pictures							
Rug							
Table							
Umbrella							
Vacuum Cleaner							
Other							

Laundry Room

	Cost/Year Purchased	Month/Year First Used in Business	Cost or Fair Market Value When First Used in Business	Percentage of Business Use (Choose only one)			Year Disposed
				T/S%	100% Business	Actual Business %	
Cabinets							
Chair							
Dehumidifier							
Dryer							
Electric iron							
Fan							
Freezer							
Ironing board							
Sewing machine							
Table							
Tub							
Vacuum cleaner							
Washing machine							
Other							

Basement

	Cost/Year Purchased	Month/Year First Used in Business	Cost or Fair Market Value When First Used in Business	Percentage of Business Use (Choose only one)		Year Disposed
				T/S%	100% Business	Actual Business %	
Chair							
Dehumidifier							
Dryer							
Fireplace wood							
Freezer							
Hand tools							
Heating unit							
Holiday decorations							
Ladder							
Power tools							
Refrigerator							
Rugs							
Shelving							
Tables							
Washing machine							
Workbench							

Deck/Porch/Back Yard

	Cost/Year Purchased	Month/Year First Used in Business	Cost or Fair Market Value When First Used in Business	Percentage of Business Use (Choose only one)			Year Disposed
				T/S%	100% Business	Actual Business %	
Barbecue							
Grill							
Lawn furniture							
Outdoor shed							
Picnic table							
Playground equipment							
Porch/deck furniture							
Sand box							
Swing set							
Toys							
Other							

Garage/Storage Shed

Note on vehicles: Providers may claim expenses for their vehicles using a standard mileage method or an actual expenses method. See the latest *Family Child Care Tax Workbook and Organizer* for details.

	Cost/Year Purchased	Month/Year First Used in Business	Cost or Fair Market Value When First Used in Business	Percentage of Business Use (Choose only one)			Year Disposed
				T/S%	*100% Business*	*Actual Business %*	
Bicycles							
Chair							
Fireplace wood							
Freezer							
Garbage can							
Garden hose							
Garden tools							
Hedger							
Ladder							
Lawn furniture							
Lawn games							
Lawn mower							
Painting materials							
Power tools							
Snow blower							
Snow shovel							

Spreader	Sprinklers	Tiller	Tools	Vehicle #1	Vehicle #2	Vehicle #3	Wheelbarrow	Other													

Attic/Storage Areas

	Cost/Year Purchased	Month/Year First Used in Business	Cost or Fair Market Value When First Used in Business	Percentage of Business Use (Choose only one)		Year Disposed
				T/S%	*100% Business*	*Actual Business %*
Lawn Furniture						
Holiday decorations						
Toys in rotation						
Other						

Other Room

| Cost/Year Purchased | Month/Year First Used in Business | Cost or Fair Market Value When First Used in Business | Percentage of Business Use (Choose only one) | | Year Disposed |
			T/S%	100% Business	Actual Business %	

Other Room

| Cost/Year Purchased | Month/Year First Used in Business | Cost or Fair Market Value When First Used in Business | Percentage of Business Use (Choose only one) | | | Year Disposed |
			T/S%	100% Business	Actual Business %	

Other Room

Cost/Year Purchased	Month/Year First Used in Business	Cost or Fair Market Value When First Used in Business	Percentage of Business Use (Choose only one)			Year Disposed
			T/S%	100% Business	Actual Business %	

Other Room

Cost/Year Purchased	Month/Year First Used in Business	Cost or Fair Market Value When First Used in Business	Percentage of Business Use (Choose only one)			Year Disposed
			T/S%	100% Business	Actual Business %	

Other Room

Cost/Year Purchased	Month/Year First Used in Business	Cost or Fair Market Value When First Used in Business	Percentage of Business Use (Choose only one)			Year Disposed
			T/S%	100% Business	Actual Business %	

Summary Value of Your Items

Year_____

Total value of Time-Space Percentage items $ _____

Total value of 100% Business items $ _____

Actual Business-Use Percent items

$ _____ x _____% = $ _____

$ _____ x _____% = $ _____

$ _____ x _____% = $ _____

$ _____ x _____% = $ _____

Total Actual Business-Use Percent items $ _____

Year_____

Total value of Time-Space Percentage items $ _____

Total value of 100% Business items $ _____

Actual Business-Use Percent items

$ _____ x _____% = $ _____

$ _____ x _____% = $ _____

$ _____ x _____% = $ _____

$ _____ x _____% = $ _____

Total Actual Business-Use Percent items $ _____

Year_____

Total value of Time-Space Percentage items $ _____

Total value of 100% Business items $ _____

Actual Business-Use Percent items

$ _____ x _____% = $ _____

$ _____ x _____% = $ _____

$ _____ x _____% = $ _____

$ _____ x _____% = $ _____

Total Actual Business-Use Percent items $ _____

Year_____

Total value of Time-Space Percentage items $ _____

Total value of 100% Business items $ _____

Actual Business-Use Percent items

$ _____ x _____% = $ _____

$ _____ x _____% = $ _____

$ _____ x _____% = $ _____

$ _____ x _____% = $ _____

Total Actual Business-Use Percent items $ _____

Home/Home Improvements/Land Improvements

This section allows you to list your home, home improvements, and land improvements so that you can depreciate them on your tax return. List your home on the special section on the next page. A home improvement is something that increases the value of your home or prolongs its useful life and lasts longer than a year. Examples include a new roof, a new furnace, remodeling the kitchen or family room, adding on a new room, a new deck, and new built-in appliances. A land improvement increases the value of your land (fence, new driveway and so on). Save receipts of your home and land improvement projects and take pictures once they are completed. For details on how to claim depreciation on these projects, see the latest edition of the *Family Child Care Tax Workbook and Organizer*. For a comprehensive listing of home and land improvements, see the *Family Child Care Record-Keeping Guide*.

Make separate lists in the *Inventory-Keeper* for home and land improvements completed before your business began and those completed after your business began. Total the improvements completed before your business began. These will be added to the cost of your home in calculating your home depreciation deduction. Improvements completed after your business began should be depreciated as separate items.

A repair or maintenance is something that helps retain the value of the home. Examples include fixing a broken window, replacing roof shingles, and cleaning the furnace. Since repairs or maintenance items can be claimed as an expense in the year completed, do not report them on the *Inventory-Keeper*.

For projects completed after your business began, see page 5 to learn how to fill out the Percentage of Business Use.

Home

Home address _____

_____

_____

Year purchased   _____

Purchase price of home $_____

Subtract the value of the land at
    the time of purchase   - $_____

Add the value of the improvements to
    your home and land completed before
    your business began. Take this amount
    from the total cost of projects in the
    chart below   + $_____

The total is your home's business value $_____

Home and Land Improvements Completed Before Your Business Began

Description of Project	Month/Year Completed	Cost of Project
_____	_____	_____
_____	_____	_____
_____	_____	_____
_____	_____	_____
_____	_____	_____
_____	_____	_____
_____	_____	_____
_____	_____	_____
_____	_____	_____
_____	_____	_____
_____	_____	_____
_____	_____	_____
_____	_____	_____
_____	_____	_____

Total cost of all projects completed
    before your business began $_____

Home and Land Improvements Completed After Your Business Began

Description of Project	Month/Year Completed	Cost of Project	Percentage of Business Use (Choose only one)			Year Disposed
			T/S%	100% Business	Actual Business %	

Sample List of Strictly Personal Items

Antiques
Art objects
Auto equipment
Beds
Books
Bric-a-brac
Buffet
Bureau/dresser
CDs/cassettes/records
Chandelier
Chest
Children's clothing
    blouses
    coats
    dresses
    hats
    jackets
    overcoats
    pants
    raincoats
    shirts
    shoes
    slacks
    suits
    sweaters
China
    breakfast sets
    dinnerware
    luncheon sets
    serving pieces
Cosmetics
Crystal
    bowls/vases
    cocktail glasses
    decanters
    dishes

    glasses/tumblers
    pitchers
    punch bowl sets
Dressing table
DVD player
Electric coffee maker
Figurines
Glassware cabinet
Hair dryer
Hobby collections
Jewelry and furs
    bracelets
    brooches/pins
    earrings
    furs
    necklaces
    rings
    watches
Linens
Liquors/wines
Luggage
Medicines
Men's clothing
    coats
    formal wear
    hats
    neckties
    pants
    outer jackets
    raincoats
    shirts
    shoes
    sport jackets
    suits
    sweaters
Paintings

Power tools
Silverware
Sporting equipment or
leisure items
    art supplies
    bicycles
    boating equipment
    bowling equipment
    camping equipment
    exercise equipment
    fishing tackle
    golf clubs
    guns/firearms
    hunting equipment
    photography
      equipment
    ski equipment
    tennis equipment
Storage trunks
Television
Toilet articles
Towels
Women's clothing
    blouses
    coats
    dresses
    handbags
    hats
    jackets
    lingerie
    raincoats
    shoes
    skirts
    slacks
    suits
    sweaters

Table for Strictly Personal Items

Item	Month/Year Purchased	Purchase Price	Serial#	Room

Table for Strictly Personal Items

Item	Month/Year Purchased	Purchase Price	Serial#	Room

Table for Strictly Personal Items

Item	Month/Year Purchased	Purchase Price	Serial#	Room

Table for Strictly Personal Items

Item	Month/Year Purchased	Purchase Price	Serial#	Room